Cool Clay Projects

Pam Scheunemann

ABDO
Publishing Company

visit us at
www.abdopub.com

Published by ABDO Publishing Company, 4940 Viking Drive, Edina, Minnesota 55435. Copyright ©
2005 by Abdo Consulting Group, Inc. International copyrights reserved in all countries. No part of this
book may be reproduced in any form without written permission from the publisher. Checkerboard Library
is a trademark and logo of ABDO Publishing Company.

Printed in the United States.

Design and Production: Mighty Media, Inc.
    Cover Photo: Anders Hanson
    Interior Photos: Anders Hanson
    Series Coordinator: Pam Scheunemann
    Editor: Pam Price
    Art Direction: Pam Scheunemann

Library of Congress Cataloging-in-Publication Data

Scheunemann, Pam, 1955-
    Cool clay projects / Pam Scheunemann.
      p. cm. -- (Cool crafts)
    ISBN 1-59197-740-1
    1. Polymer clay craft--Juvenile literature. I. Title. II. Series.

TT297.S298 2004
731.4'2--dc22
                                               2004053119

For Your Safety
Some of the tools shown in this book should be used only when an adult is present. All clay
projects must be baked in the oven. Always have an adult present when you use the oven.

Contents

Introduction 4

About Polymer Clay 6

Tools & Equipment 8

Conditioning the Clay 13

Color Mixing 14

Millefiori 16

Playful Pens 18

Double-Dot Beads 22

Funky Frames 26

Fresh Flowerpots 28

Glossary 31

Index 32

Boldfaced words throughout the text are defined in the glossary.

Introduction

People have used clay to create functional and decorative objects for centuries. There's nothing new about that. What is new is that there is now a man-made alternative to traditional mixtures of earthen materials. That alternative is polymer clay.

Polymer clay is made of very fine plastic particles combined with a plasticizer to make the clay soft. Like traditional clay, you can mold, carve, and sculpt polymer clay. And also like traditional clay, you heat it to cure, or harden, it. However, polymer clay can be fired in a regular home oven or toaster oven. Traditional clay must be fired in a kiln.

Polymer clay has many benefits. It can be made to resemble fabric, stone, or even metal. Polymer clay comes in many colors, which you can mix to create your own colors. It retains its vibrant color after firing. It does not shrink during baking.

Young or old, everyone can work with polymer clay. Compared to other crafts, it is relatively inexpensive and requires very few tools. Projects can be created using things from around the house.

This book will teach you the basic techniques of working with polymer clay. With those techniques, you can make the simple projects shown in the book. From there, the only limit to what you can create is your imagination!

About Polymer Clay

Working with polymer clay is very fun. But before you dive in, there are some things you should know about handling, baking, and storing your clay.

Safety

Polymer clay is nontoxic to touch, but should not be eaten. Nor should it come into contact with food. Once a utensil or container has touched polymer clay, it should never be used for food preparation or storage. Any tools you use should be dedicated to clay.

If you make bowls or dishes from the clay, use them only for decorative purposes. Do not serve food in them. Food should not come into contact with baked or unbaked clay. After working with clay, always wash your hands with soap.

Some colors of clay may stain surfaces, clothing, or carpeting. The stain can usually be removed with warm, soapy water. Some colors of clay, such as red, will stain your hands. Wash your hands after working with these clays. Then you will not contaminate the next color you work with.

Wash your hands thoroughly after working with polymer clay. If it is hard to remove, try washing with baking soda.

Baking

The plastics in the clay need to reach a certain temperature to cure. Be sure to follow the manufacturer's instructions for oven temperature and baking time. When your project is ready to be baked, have an adult work with you. You can use either an oven or a toaster oven. Never use a microwave.

Most brands of clay should be baked at 275 degrees (135°C). Use an oven thermometer to check your oven's temperature. The temperature setting on the dial does not always accurately display the oven temperature. It's important to bake clay at the correct temperature. If baked at temperatures exceeding 300 degrees (149°C), the clay may burn and emit harmful gases.

Use a timer to be sure you don't cook the clay too long. Once the time is up, just turn the oven off and let your clay cool down naturally. Or, simply remove it from the oven. The clay is not done hardening until it is completely cool. Wait until it is cool before you handle it.

Bake clay on a clean, smooth surface. The clay will pick up any pattern it comes into contact with. You can use an old, metal cookie sheet or cake pan or a glass pie or cake pan. Line the pan with baking parchment. That will keep the clay from getting shiny spots where it touches the pan.

Storage

Store polymer clay in a cool, dark place. Wrap your extra clay in plastic wrap, then store it in an airtight container. The clay contains a plasticizer that can harm some surfaces it comes into contact with. If you use a plastic container, be sure the clay doesn't come into contact with it. The plasticizer may actually fuse with the plastic container.

Tools & Equipment

You will mostly use your hands to work with polymer clay, but there are other tools you will find useful. Some are made specifically for use with polymer clay. Others you can find around the house. Things like a toothpick or a piece of screen can be terrific tools.

Remember that you can never use a tool for food preparation once you've used it for clay work. Always ask permission before using kitchen items such as cutting boards, knives, cookie cutters, and baking sheets for clay work.

Work Surface

You will need a clean work surface that is flat and smooth. Good options are a glass or melamine cutting board, a piece of Formica, or a cookie sheet. Do not use a wooden or **porous** surface as the clay can damage it. Tape a sheet of waxed paper over your work surface to keep it clean. Then you can easily switch to a clean piece for each color of clay you use.

Rolling Tools

Various types of rolling tools are very useful when working with clay. They can be used to **condition** or smooth clay or to make flat sheets of clay. You can use a Lucite roller, a printer's brayer, an old drinking glass, or a jar.

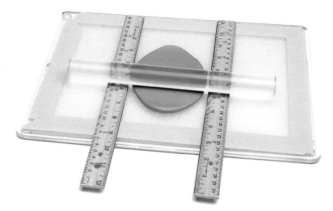

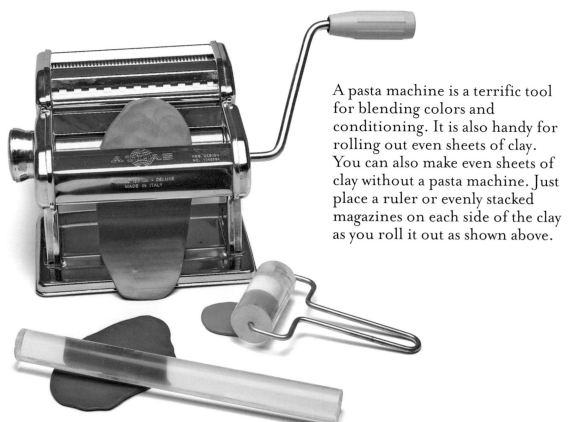

A pasta machine is a terrific tool for blending colors and conditioning. It is also handy for rolling out even sheets of clay. You can also make even sheets of clay without a pasta machine. Just place a ruler or evenly stacked magazines on each side of the clay as you roll it out as shown above.

Cutting Tools

You cut clay into small, workable pieces with a butter knife. But you need a sharper blade to cut slices from **canes** without distorting the pattern. Options include a single-edge razor blade, a blade made for cutting polymer clay, or a craft knife. These blades are very sharp, so you must have an adult help you use them.

The longer clay-slicing blades are good for cutting long strips of clay. You can make them a bit safer by pressing a ball of clay on each corner of the dull side. Bake the blade. Now you have handles showing you the safe side to pick up.

Shape cutters are available where you purchase clay and are made specifically for use with clay. They come in many shapes and sizes. Kemper cutters have a spring-loaded plunger that pushes the clay out after cutting. You can also use cookie cutters.

Piercing and Sculpting Tools

Some projects require piercing a hole in the clay. Just about any item with a sharp point can be used. Toothpicks, darning needles, bamboo skewers, and heavy wire are all options. You can also find inexpensive metal rods at hobby and hardware stores. When making beads, make sure the hole is large enough to accommodate the cord you plan to use.

Many items can be used to sculpt the clay. You can use the end of a paintbrush to make indentations or draw a pattern in your clay. A needle can make marks that look like quilt stitching.

Texturing clay can be really fun too. Just find something with a great texture or pattern, perhaps a piece of window screen or a paper doily. Press or roll it into the clay, then remove it to reveal the pattern.

Use push molds to easily create detailed, three-dimensional shapes. They come in many different shapes and are often available where you purchase your clay.

Measuring Tools

Sometimes you may want to cut several pieces of clay to the same length. You can use a ruler or you can stick pieces of masking tape to the work surface to measure even pieces. There is a six-sided measuring tool called Marxit™. It has raised marks in different increments on each side. You just press it into the clay to mark equal parts for cutting.

Glue

Sometime you will need to use glue to adhere clay to a surface. Tacky Glue® and Sobo® Glue are nontoxic craft glues. They work well for attaching clay to **porous** and nonporous surfaces.

Conditioning the Clay

In order to work with the clay, it needs to be soft and pliable, not crumbling. Getting the clay to this workable state is called **conditioning**. There are several brands of polymer clay, and they differ in their degree of hardness. Some clay is made with an additive that softens the clay. This affects how much conditioning the clay will need.

Fimo® Soft, Premo! Sculpey®, and Sculpey III® are the three clays best suited for the projects in this book. These clays are relatively easy to condition. They will maintain their shape and color when reducing a patterned **cane** of clay.

To condition clay, first cut off a small piece of clay and roll it into a ball. Then roll it into a log between your palms. The heat from your hands helps to soften the clay. Fold the log of clay and repeat the process until the clay becomes pliable.

You can also roll the clay with a roller to help condition it. Running the clay through a pasta machine several times also helps condition it.

Fully conditioned clay will stretch without immediately breaking. It will also have a slightly spongy feel. If it gets too soft, put it in the refrigerator or just let it sit for a while.

If the clay feels hard and you are using Sculpey or Premo!, try adding some Sculpey clay softner. If you're using Fimo Soft, try some Fimo Mix Quick to assist in conditioning the clay.

Color Mixing

Polymer clay comes in many colors. The three primary colors are red, yellow, and blue. These three colors can be mixed to make many other colors.

Primary Colors

These colors cannot be made by mixing other colors.

How to Mix Colors

Condition and roll out a log of each color you want to mix. Twist the logs together. Continue to knead the clay until the color is well blended. When you mix your own colors, always start with the lighter color and add in the darker color. Try some of your own color combinations. Write the mixtures down so you can duplicate the color later.

Secondary Colors

These colors can be made by mixing equal amounts of two primary colors.

Tints and Shades

A tint is a lighter version of a color made by adding that color to white. A shade is a darker version of a color made by adding black. For example, adding red to white creates pink. Adding black to red creates maroon.

Marbling

Twist logs of two or more colors together.

Roll the logs together and fold the log in half. Twisting the logs will increase the marbled pattern. Continue rolling and folding. Stop when you get a pattern you like. Do not mix too much or you'll make a solid color.

Marbled clay can be rolled flat. This really shows the marbling well.

Millefiori

Millefiori is a technique developed by Venetian glass makers. They would combine and stretch rods of molten glass to make a cylinder, or **cane**, with the same pattern running its entire length. They would apply slices of the cane to beads or other glass objects, creating the look of many flowers. That's where the name comes from. *Millefiori* means "a thousand flowers" in Italian.

Polymer clay is an excellent medium for creating similar patterns because the colors don't distort when the cane is stretched, or **reduced**.

Bull's-Eye Cane

Roll out a log, or snake, of one color for the center. Make a flat sheet of another color. Wrap the sheet around the log, cutting it where the edges meet. Smooth the cut edges.

You can shape a bull's-eye cane into a triangular or square log using your roller.

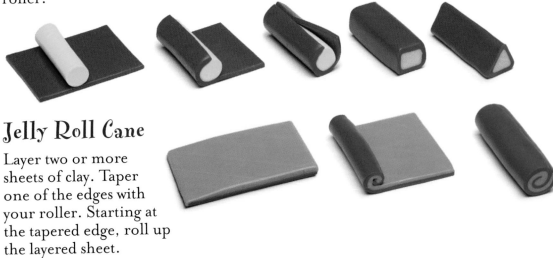

Jelly Roll Cane

Layer two or more sheets of clay. Taper one of the edges with your roller. Starting at the tapered edge, roll up the layered sheet.

Checkerboard Loaves

This easy and popular pattern uses a light and a dark color.
There are two ways to make a checkerboard loaf.

Log checkerboard

Roll out logs of clay and cut them
to equal lengths. Put the logs
together in a checkerboard
pattern. Use a roller to form a
square loaf.

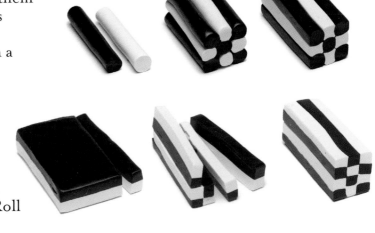

Slab checkerboard

Use two colors and make
slabs that are equal in size
and thickness. Cut lengths
that are as wide as the slab
is thick. Assemble the pieces
in a checkerboard pattern. Roll
the clay into a square loaf.

Reducing Canes and Loaves

Creating a small, intricate **millefiori cane** or loaf is easier when you assemble
it with bigger pieces of clay. Gently roll the cane with your hands or a roller
until it is much longer and thinner. This is called reducing the pattern.
Work carefully and slowly to avoid distorting the pattern.

If you like, cut the **reduced** cane into equal lengths. Put them together and
reduce the piece again. Continue this process until you get the pattern you
want.

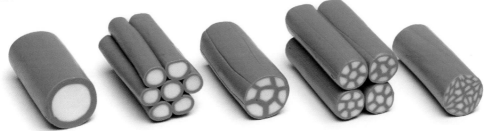

Playful Pens

These playful pens are easy to make. And, they make great gifts! Choose different clay colors and make up new **cane** patterns to totally change the look of the pens you make.

What You Need

- Polymer clay in yellow, blue, orange, turquoise, violet, and fuchsia
- Bic® Round Stic™ pen (other brands may melt in the oven)
- Small pliers with teeth
- Slicing blade
- An adult to help you slice
- Butter knife
- Wooden skewers
- Canning jar or empty metal can
- Optional: small circle cutter (the size of the top of pen barrel)

1 This **millefiori** pattern starts with a bull's-eye **cane**. Make the cane with yellow and blue clay.

2 Roll out three smaller logs each of the orange, turquoise, and violet clays. Position them around the bull's-eye cane.

3 Roll the cane, **reducing** it until you can cut it into four logs of equal length.

4 Roll five smaller logs of fuchsia. Position the four bull's-eye canes around one of the fuchsia logs. Put the other four fuchsia logs between the bull's-eye canes.

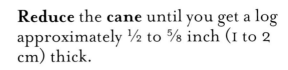

Reduce the **cane** until you get a log approximately ½ to ⅝ inch (1 to 2 cm) thick.

Using the pliers, firmly hold the metal tip of the pen. Twist the barrel until the ink cartridge comes out. Be gentle so the tip of the pen doesn't break off and leak ink. Set the ink cartridge aside, it can't go into the oven.

Cut thin slices from your cane.

Apply the slices to the pen until it's completely covered.

9 Roll the pen between your hands or on a flat surface. Do this until the slices are well blended and the clay is smooth.

10 Using a butter knife, carefully cut the **excess** clay off each end of the pen.

11 Use the circle cutter to cut a piece from a slice of **cane**. Apply this to the top of the pen and smooth the edges. Or, you can **reduce** a piece of the cane to the size of the pen top and cut a slice for the top.

12 Place the pen on a wooden skewer and rest it inside a jar or can. Bake the pen according to the clay manufacturer's instructions. When the pen is completely cool, use pliers to replace the ink cartridge.

Double-Dot Beads

Polymer clay beads are easy to make. You can make clay beads in any shape and size you like. This project includes three different bead-making techniques. The beads in this project can be used to make a necklace, a bracelet, or both!

What You Need

- Polymer clay in three contrasting colors
- Ruler or measuring tool
- Slicing blade
- An adult to help you slice
- Bamboo skewers
- Toothpick

For the Necklace

- Leather cord that fits through the holes in your beads
- Two lace end crimps
- Spring-ring clasp
- Small pliers

For the Bracelet

- Elastic cord that fits through the holes in your beads

Double-Dot Round Beads

1 Roll a log of your base bead color. Mark it off in equal sections. Cut a section and roll it into a bead. Continue cutting and making the rest of the base beads.

2 Make a bull's-eye **cane** with the other two colors. Cut thin slices of the cane and apply them **randomly** to the base bead. Roll the bead in your hands until the cane slices are smooth.

3 Gently pierce the bead with a toothpick. Slightly twist the toothpick as you pierce the bead.

4 Thread the beads on a bamboo skewer and bake them according to the clay manufacturer's directions.

Double-Dot Disk Beads

1 Make round base beads as in the double-dot round beads. Cut slices of the bull's-eye **cane** a bit thicker than for the round beads.

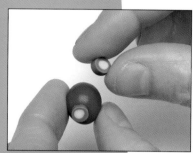

2 Apply the slices only around the middle of the base bead. Leave a little space between the slices. Gently press them into the bead without smoothing them in.

3 Hold the bead at the top and bottom and press it flat. It should be the thickness of the cane slices. Pierce the bead with a toothpick, thread it on a bamboo skewer, and bake it.

Make the Necklace

Cut a strand of leather cord twice as long as you want your necklace. String on the beads. Tie a knot next to the last bead at each end. Wrap the necklace around your neck to check the length. Trim if necessary. Put a lace end crimp on each end. Using a small pliers, press in the last ring or two of the crimp. Attach a jump ring to one end and a spring-ring clasp to the other end.

Solid-Color Filler Beads

1 Roll a fat log and pierce the center with a bamboo skewer.

2 Roll out the clay on the skewer until it is the thickness you want. If you feel the clay pulling away from the skewer, press it down firmly.

3 Use a measuring tool or ruler to make marks for cutting the log into beads. Then gently roll the log as you slice each bead. Bake the log on the skewer. When the clay is cool, remove the log from the skewer and break apart the beads.

Make the Bracelet

Wrap the elastic around your wrist twice, then cut it. String beads on the elastic to the desired length. Tie a double knot and trim the excess elastic.

Funky Frames

Create your very own pattern for a funky frame. You can use any **millefiori** pattern you can dream up. These stunning frames are perfect for framing special pictures of your family and friends.

More than Frames

You can embellish all sorts of things using this technique. Small tins, jar lids, and bottles can also be covered with cane slices.

1 To make the **millefiori** pattern shown here, make a black and white jelly roll log. Place three logs each of four colors around the outside. Then wrap the log with sheets of black, white, and then black again. **Reduce** the log.

2 To make the more detailed **cane**, cut the reduced cane into four equal pieces. Place them around a small solid-color log. Add solid-color logs between the four patterned logs. Roll the log into a square loaf while reducing it.

3 Remove the backing and glass from the frame. Cut thin slices of the patterned cane. Spread a thin layer of glue on each slice before pressing it onto the frame. Cover the frame completely. Smooth the seams using your finger or a roller.

4 Trim the **excess** clay from the front and back edges. Have an adult help you slice. Bake the frame according to the clay manufacturer's instructions. When the frame is completely cool, replace the glass and insert your favorite photo.

Fresh Flowerpots

Polymer clay can be used to embellish many household items. For this project, the clay is glued to the pot and then baked in the oven. You can use molds, shape cutters, or a patterned **cane** to make a fresh flowerpot.

What You Need

- ▸ Polymer clay
- ▸ All-purpose glue
- ▸ Toothpicks
- ▸ Flowerpot and saucer

For the Push Mold

- ▸ Flexible push mold
- ▸ Pencil with eraser

For the Cutout

- ▸ Clay cutter in flower or other shape

Push Mold Project

1 Select colors for your push mold pattern. If you use more than one color, layer the colors. First roll a ball that fits into the deepest part of the mold. Press it in with a pencil eraser.

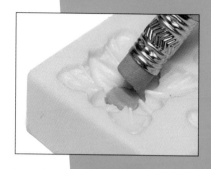

2 Add the next color or colors the same way. The clay should be even with the top of the mold. If it is slightly domed, push the clay in with your finger. Remove any **excess** clay. Make a few practice molds to get the hang of it.

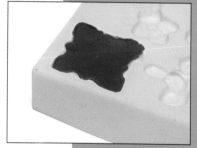

3 Place the mold in the freezer for a couple of minutes. Then hold the mold upside down and release the molded clay. Press on the back of the mold and the clay should pop out like an ice cube.

4 When all your molded pieces are done, you are ready to glue. Spread some glue on a paper plate. Use a toothpick to spread a thin layer of glue on the clay.

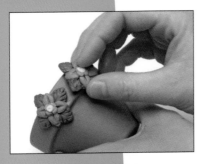

5 Attach the molded clay to the flowerpot. After you've attached all the clay pieces, trim off the clay that sticks up above the rim of the pot. Bake the pot in the oven according to the clay manufacturer's directions.

Cutout Project

1 **Condition** the clay and roll out a flat sheet. Use a cutter to cut out the flower shapes.

2 Roll out a small **cane** of clay. Cut a slice for the center of each flower.

3 Place the dots on the flowers. Follow steps four and five from the push mold project to complete your flowerpot.

Glossary

cane - a log of clay made up of various patterns and colors.

condition - to make ready for use.

excess - more than the specified or needed amount.

millefiori - a decoration made by cutting slices from a multicolored cane. Italian for "a thousand flowers."

porous - full of pores and therefore able to absorb fluids.

random - having no specific plan or pattern.

reduce - to decrease in size, amount, or number. In clay work, to roll a multi-colored, patterned cane in order to reduce the size of the cane and its pattern.

Web Sites

To learn more about polymer clay, visit ABDO Publishing Company on the World Wide Web at **www.abdopub.com**. Web sites about polymer clay are featured on our Book Links page. These links are routinely monitored and updated to provide the most current information available.

Index

B

baking 5, 6, 7
baking parchment 7
bull's-eye cane 16, 19, 23, 24

C

checkerboard loaves 17
color mixing 14
conditioning 9, 13, 31
cookie cutters 8, 10
cutout project 30
cutting board 8
cutting tools 10

F

flowerpots 28
food 6, 8
frames 26

G

glue 12, 27, 29

J

jelly roll cane 16

L

Lucite roller 9

M

marbling 15
measuring tools 12
millefiori 16, 17, 26, 27, 31

O

oven 4, 6, 7, 30

P

pasta machine 9, 13
pens 18
piercing and sculpting tools 11
plasticizer 4, 7
polymer clay beads 22
primary colors 14, 15
push molds 11, 29, 30

R

reducing canes and loaves 17, 19, 27, 31
rolling tools 9

S

safety 6
screen 8, 11
secondary colors 15
shape cutters 10, 28
storage 6, 7

T

texturing clay 11
toaster oven 4, 6

W

waxed paper 8
work surface 8